The Cookout Salad Cookbook

Delicious Salad Recipes for Summer Cookouts, Picnics, and Outdoor Events

By
BookSumo Press

Published by
BookSumo Press, a DBA of Saxonberg Associates
http://www.booksumo.com/

ABOUT THE AUTHOR.

BookSumo Press is a publisher of unique, easy, and healthy cookbooks.

Our cookbooks span all topics and all subjects. If you want a deep dive into the possibilities of cooking with any type of ingredient. Then BookSumo Press is your go to place for robust yet simple and delicious cookbooks and recipes. Whether you are looking for great tasting pressure cooker recipes or authentic ethic and cultural food. BookSumo Press has a delicious and easy cookbook for you.

With simple ingredients, and even simpler step-by-step instructions BookSumo cookbooks get everyone in the kitchen chefing delicious meals.

BookSumo is an independent publisher of books operating in the beautiful Garden State (NJ) and our team of chefs and kitchen experts are here to teach, eat, and be merry!

INTRODUCTION

Welcome to *The Effortless Chef Series*! Thank you for taking the time to purchase this cookbook.

Come take a journey into the delights of easy cooking. The point of this cookbook and all BookSumo Press cookbooks is to exemplify the effortless nature of cooking simply.

In this book we focus on Cookout Salad. You will find that even though the recipes are simple, the taste of the dishes are quite amazing.

So will you take an adventure in simple cooking? If the answer is yes please consult the table of contents to find the dishes you are most interested in.

Once you are ready, jump right in and start cooking.

— BookSumo Press

TABLE OF CONTENTS

Any Issues? Contact Us

If you find that something important to you is missing from this book please contact us at info@booksumo.com.

We will take your concerns into consideration when the 2nd edition of this book is published. And we will keep you updated!

— BookSumo Press

Legal Notes

Common Abbreviations

cup(s)	C.
tablespoon	tbsp
teaspoon	tsp
ounce	oz.
pound	lb

*All units used are standard American measurements

Chapter 1: Easy Cookout Salad Recipes

Feta-Farfalle Pasta Salad

Ingredients

- 1 (12 ounce) package farfalle pasta
- 10 ounces baby spinach, rinsed and torn into bite-size piece
- 2 ounces crumbled feta cheese with basil and tomato
- 1 red onion, chopped
- 1 (15 ounce) can black olives, drained and chopped
- 1 cup Italian-style salad dressing
- 4 cloves garlic, minced
- 1 lemon, juiced
- 1/2 tsp garlic salt
- 1/2 tsp ground black pepper

Directions

- Cook pasta in salty boiling water for about 10 minutes until tender before draining it.
- Coat a mixture of pasta, olives, spinach, red onion and cheese with a mixture of salad dressing, pepper, lemon juice, salt and garlic very thoroughly before refrigerating it for at least two hours.

- Serve.

Serving: 6

Timing Information:

Preparation	Cooking	Total Time
10 mins	15 mins	2 hrs 25 mins

Nutritional Information:

Calories	334 kcal
Carbohydrates	41.8 g
Cholesterol	6 mg
Fat	16.6 g
Fiber	4.8 g
Protein	8.6 g
Sodium	1167 mg

* Percent Daily Values are based on a 2,000 calorie diet.

CAESAR PARMESAN PASTA SALAD

Ingredients

- 1 (16 ounce) package rotini pasta
- 1 cup Italian-style salad dressing
- 1 cup creamy Caesar salad dressing
- 1 cup grated Parmesan cheese
- 1 red bell pepper, diced
- 1 green bell pepper, chopped
- 1 red onion, diced

Directions

- Cook pasta in salty boiling water for about 10 minutes until tender before draining it.
- Mix pasta, red bell pepper, Italian salad dressing, Caesar dressing, Parmesan cheese, green bell pepper and red onion very thoroughly before refrigerating for a few hours.
- Serve.

Serving: 12
Timing Information:

Preparation	Cooking	Total Time
15 mins	15 mins	30 mins

Nutritional Information:

Calories	291 kcal
Carbohydrates	32.6 g
Cholesterol	6 mg
Fat	14.6 g
Fiber	1.8 g
Protein	8.5 g
Sodium	728 mg

* Percent Daily Values are based on a 2,000 calorie diet.

HEALTHY PASTA SALAD

Ingredients

- 1 (16 ounce) package uncooked rotini pasta
- 1 (16 ounce) bottle Italian salad dressing
- 2 cucumbers, chopped
- 6 tomatoes, chopped
- 1 bunch green onions, chopped
- 4 ounces grated Parmesan cheese
- 1 tbsp Italian seasoning

Directions

- Cook pasta in salty boiling water for about 10 minutes until tender before draining it.
- Coat a mixture of pasta, green onions, cucumbers and tomatoes with a mixture of parmesan cheese and Italian seasoning very thoroughly before refrigerating it covered for a few hours.
- Serve.

Serving: 12
Timing Information:

Preparation	Cooking	Total Time
15 mins	12 mins	30 mins

Nutritional Information:

Calories	289 kcal
Carbohydrates	34.6 g
Cholesterol	8 mg
Fat	13.9 g
Fiber	4.2 g
Protein	10 g
Sodium	764 mg

* Percent Daily Values are based on a 2,000 calorie diet.

Vegetable Pasta Salad

Ingredients

- 10 ounces fusilli pasta
- 1 onion, chopped
- 1 green bell pepper, chopped
- 2 tomatoes, chopped
- 1 cup chopped mushrooms
- 3/4 cup fat free Italian-style dressing

Directions

- Cook pasta in salty boiling water for about 10 minutes until tender before draining it.
- Mix pasta, mushrooms, onions, tomatoes and bell pepper very thoroughly before refrigerating for at least one hour.
- Serve.

Serving: 8
Timing Information:

Preparation	Cooking	Total Time
10 mins	15 mins	25 mins

Nutritional Information:

Calories	181 kcal
Carbohydrates	38.1 g
Cholesterol	0 mg
Fat	0.7 g
Fiber	2.8 g
Protein	5.4 g
Sodium	238 mg

* Percent Daily Values are based on a 2,000 calorie diet.

Grilled Pasta Salad

Ingredients

- 4 skinless, boneless chicken breast halves
- steak seasoning to taste
- 8 ounces rotini pasta
- 8 ounces mozzarella cheese, cubed
- 1 red onion, chopped
- 1 head romaine lettuce, chopped
- 6 cherry tomatoes, chopped

Directions

- At first you need to set grill at medium heat and put some oil before starting anything else.
- Coat chicken breast with steak seasoning before cooking it on the preheated grill for 8 minutes each side.
- Cook pasta in salty boiling water for about 10 minutes until tender before draining it.
- Add mixture of tomatoes, cheese, onion and lettuce into the bowl containing pasta and chicken.
- Mix it thoroughly before serving.

Serving: 4
Timing Information:

Preparation	Cooking	Total Time
15 mins	30 mins	45 mins

Nutritional Information:

Calories	504 kcal
Carbohydrates	48 g
Cholesterol	103 mg
Fat	13.2 g
Fiber	4.4 g
Protein	46.5 g
Sodium	650 mg

* Percent Daily Values are based on a 2,000 calorie diet.

Italian Chicken Pasta Salad

Ingredients

- 1 cup seashell pasta
- 1 cup chopped, cooked chicken meat
- 3 green onions, chopped into 1 inch pieces
- 1 red bell pepper, chopped
- 1 cup sliced black olives
- 1 cucumber, peeled and chopped
- 2/3 cup Italian-style salad dressing
- 1/4 cup sunflower seeds(optional)

Directions

- Cook pasta in salty boiling water for about 10 minutes until tender before draining it.
- Coat mixture of pasta, bell pepper, chicken, green onions, olives and cucumber with dressing very thoroughly before refrigerating for at least 2 hours.
- Serve.

Serving: 6
Timing Information:

Preparation	Cooking	Total Time
10 mins	15 mins	2 hrs 25 mins

Nutritional Information:

Calories	218 kcal
Carbohydrates	20.4 g
Cholesterol	18 mg
Fat	11.4 g
Fiber	2.2 g
Protein	9.6 g
Sodium	654 mg

* Percent Daily Values are based on a 2,000 calorie diet.

THE BEST ITALIAN PASTA SALAD I

Ingredients

- 1 (12 ounce) package tri-color rotini pasta
- 3/4 pound Italian salami, finely diced
- 1/2 green bell pepper, sliced
- 1/2 red bell pepper, sliced
- 1/2 red onion, chopped
- 1 cup Italian-style salad dressing
- 1 (6 ounce) can sliced black olives
- 8 ounces small fresh mozzarella balls (ciliegine)
- 3 (.7 ounce) packages dry Italian-style salad dressing mix, or to taste
- 1/2 cup shredded Parmesan cheese

Directions

- Cook pasta in salty boiling water for about 10 minutes until tender before draining it.
- Coat mixture of pasta, red bell pepper, salami, green bell pepper, onion, salad dressing, olives, and mozzarella cheese with dry salad dressing very thoroughly before refrigerating for at least 2 hours.
- Sprinkle some parmesan cheese before serving.

Serving: 12
Timing Information:

Preparation	Cooking	Total Time
15 mins	10 mins	25 mins

Nutritional Information:

Calories	371 kcal
Carbohydrates	29.2 g
Cholesterol	46 mg
Fat	21 g
Fiber	1.6 g
Protein	15.2 g
Sodium	1893 mg

* Percent Daily Values are based on a 2,000 calorie diet.

South American Pasta Salad

Ingredients

- 2 cups spiral pasta
- 1 pound ground beef
- 1 (1.25 ounce) package taco seasoning
- 3 cups shredded lettuce
- 2 cups halved cherry tomatoes
- 1 cup shredded Cheddar cheese
- 1/2 cup chopped onion
- 1/2 cup French salad dressing
- 1 (7 ounce) bag corn chips
- 2 tbsps sour cream

Directions

- Cook pasta in salty boiling water for about 10 minutes until tender before draining it.
- Cook ground beef in a large skillet for about 10 minutes or until you see that it is no longer pink from the center before stirring in taco seasoning.
- Coat mixture of pasta and beef with mixture lettuce, French dressing, tomatoes, Cheddar cheese, onion and corn chips very thoroughly before refrigerating for at least 2 hours.
- Add some sour cream at the top before serving.

Serving: 6
Timing Information:

Preparation	Cooking	Total Time
10 mins	20 mins	40 mins

Nutritional Information:

Calories	618 kcal
Carbohydrates	46.4 g
Cholesterol	68 mg
Fat	38.4 g
Fiber	3.5 g
Protein	22.8 g
Sodium	980 mg

* Percent Daily Values are based on a 2,000 calorie diet.

Linguine Romano Pasta Salad

Ingredients

- 1 (8 ounce) package linguine pasta
- 1 (12 ounce) bag broccoli florets, cut into bite-size pieces
- 1/4 cup olive oil
- 4 tsps minced garlic
- 1/2 tsp red pepper flakes
- 1/2 cup finely shredded Romano cheese
- 2 tbsps finely chopped fresh flat-leaf parsley
- 1/4 tsp ground black pepper
- salt to taste

Directions

- Cook linguine in salty boiling water for about 10 minutes until tender before draining it.
- Steam broccoli for about 5 minutes with the help of steamer insert in a saucepan.
- Cook garlic and red pepper flakes in hot oil for about 3 minutes before adding this and broccoli to the pot containing linguine.
- Stir in Romano cheese, salt, parsley and black pepper.
- Combine thoroughly before serving.

Serving: 6

Timing Information:

Preparation	Cooking	Total Time
15 mins	20 mins	35 mins

Nutritional Information:

Calories	275 kcal
Carbohydrates	32.2 g
Cholesterol	10 mg
Fat	12.8 g
Fiber	2.9 g
Protein	9.9 g
Sodium	141 mg

* Percent Daily Values are based on a 2,000 calorie diet.

Rotini Cucumber Pasta Salad

Ingredients

- 14 ounces uncooked rotini pasta
- 2 cucumbers, chopped
- 1/2 onion, finely chopped
- 10 cherry tomatoes, quartered
- 3/4 cup pitted black olives, sliced
- 1 cup Italian-style salad dressing

Directions

- Cook rotini in salty boiling water for about 10 minutes until tender before draining it.
- Coat a mixture of pasta, olives, cucumbers, tomatoes and onion with Italian dressing very thoroughly before refrigerating for at least two hours.
- Serve.

Serving: 8
Timing Information:

Preparation	Cooking	Total Time
15 mins	15 mins	2 hrs 30 mins

Nutritional Information:

Calories	297 kcal
Carbohydrates	43.9 g
Cholesterol	0 mg
Fat	10.6 g
Fiber	2.6 g
Protein	7.2 g
Sodium	608 mg

* Percent Daily Values are based on a 2,000 calorie diet.

California Mexican Pasta Salad

Ingredients

- 1 (16 ounce) package tri-color rotini pasta
- 1 (15 ounce) can black beans, drained and rinsed
- 1 (11 ounce) can Mexican-style corn, drained
- 1 (4 ounce) can chopped green chilies
- 1/2 cup chopped red bell pepper
- 1/2 cup Italian-style salad dressing, or more to taste
- 1/2 cup shredded Mexican cheese blend
- 3 green onions, thinly sliced
- 1/3 cup minced fresh cilantro
- 1 slice onion, minced
- 2 tbsps taco seasoning mix
- 1/2 lime, juiced

Directions

- Cook rotini in salty boiling water for about 10 minutes until tender before draining it.
- Coat rotini with a mixture of black beans, taco seasoning, corn, Mexican cheese, green chilies, green onions, red bell pepper, Italian dressing, cilantro, onion, and lime juice very thoroughly before refrigerating for at least two hours.
- Serve.

Serving: 12

Timing Information:

Preparation	Cooking	Total Time
15 mins	10 mins	25 mins

Nutritional Information:

Calories	653 kcal
Carbohydrates	66.9 g
Cholesterol	63 mg
Fat	31.7 g
Fiber	8.1 g
Protein	28 g
Sodium	902 mg

* Percent Daily Values are based on a 2,000 calorie diet.

Easy Corkscrew Pasta Salad

Ingredients

- 1 (12 ounce) package rotini/corkscrew pasta
- 1 (16 ounce) package frozen mixed vegetables, thawed
- 1 (15.25 ounce) can kidney beans, drained
- 1 1/2 cups finely chopped celery
- 1 cucumber - peeled, seeded and chopped
- 1/2 cup finely chopped green bell pepper
- 1/2 cup finely chopped onion
- 2/3 cup cider vinegar
- 2 tbsps margarine
- 2/3 cup sugar
- 1 tbsp all-purpose flour
- 1/2 tsp salt
- 1 tbsp prepared brown mustard

Directions

- Bring a mixture of vinegar, flour, margarine, sugar, salt and brown mustard to boil and cook for 5 minutes.
- Coat mixture of cooked pasta, cucumber, mixed vegetables, kidney beans, celery, green pepper and onion with this dressing very thoroughly before refrigerating it for at least an hour.
- Serve.

Serving: 12
Timing Information:

Preparation	Cooking	Total Time
15 mins	10 mins	25 mins

Nutritional Information:

Calories	170 kcal
Carbohydrates	32.8 g
Cholesterol	0 mg
Fat	2.5 g
Fiber	4.6 g
Protein	5.3 g
Sodium	243 mg

* Percent Daily Values are based on a 2,000 calorie diet.

Tri-Color Pasta Salad

Ingredients

- 1 (16 ounce) package tri-color pasta
- 2/3 cup olive oil
- 3 tbsps white wine vinegar
- 1/4 cup fresh basil leaves
- 2 tbsps grated Parmesan cheese
- 1 1/4 tsps salt
- 1/4 tsp ground black pepper
- 1 red bell pepper, cut into strips
- 1 yellow bell pepper, cut into strips
- 1 orange bell pepper, cut into strips
- 1 medium fresh tomato, chopped
- 1 (2.25 ounce) can black olives, drained
- 8 ounces mozzarella cheese, cubed

Directions

- Cook pasta in salty boiling water for about 10 minutes until tender before draining it.
- Blend olive oil, Parmesan cheese, white wine vinegar, basil, salt, and pepper in a food processor very thoroughly before mixing it with pasta, red bell pepper, yellow bell pepper, orange bell pepper, tomato, and olives.
- Sprinkle some mozzarella cheese before serving.

Serving: 8
Timing Information:

Preparation	Cooking	Total Time
15 mins	10 mins	25 mins

Nutritional Information:

Calories	483 kcal
Carbohydrates	48 g
Cholesterol	19 mg
Fat	25.2 g
Fiber	3.6 g
Protein	16.2 g
Sodium	631 mg

* Percent Daily Values are based on a 2,000 calorie diet.

Garbanzo Bow-Tie Pasta Salad

Ingredients

- 1 (15 ounce) can garbanzo beans, drained
- 1 (13.75 ounce) can artichoke hearts, drained and diced
- 1 1/2 cups frozen green peas
- 1/2 cup diced black olives
- 1/2 red onion, diced
- 1 (16 ounce) package farfalle (bow tie) pasta
- 1 1/2 cups diced queso blanco cheese
- 1 (12 ounce) bottle Italian-style salad dressing
- cracked black pepper to taste

Directions

- Cook pasta in salty boiling water for about 10 minutes until tender before draining it.
- Coat a mixture of pasta, garbanzo beans, artichoke hearts, frozen peas, queso blanco cheese, black olives, and red onion with Italian salad dressing very thoroughly before adding cracked black pepper.
- Set it aside for about 5 minutes before serving.

Serving: 12
Timing Information:

Preparation	Cooking	Total Time
15 mins	15 mins	35 mins

Nutritional Information:

Calories	399 kcal
Carbohydrates	52.9 g
Cholesterol	12 mg
Fat	15.3 g
Fiber	5.4 g
Protein	14.6 g
Sodium	1042 mg

* Percent Daily Values are based on a 2,000 calorie diet.

Ravioli & Broccoli Pasta Salad

Ingredients

- 2 (9 ounce) packages Refrigerated Cheese Ravioli, cooked, chilled
- 1/4 cup extra virgin olive oil
- 4 large cloves garlic, finely chopped
- 1/4 cup red wine vinegar
- 2 medium tomatoes, chopped
- 2 cups broccoli florets
- 1 large green bell pepper, chopped
- 1/2 cup pitted and halved ripe olives
- 1/2 cup Refrigerated Parmesan
- 1/4 cup Refrigerated Romano Cheese

Directions

- Cook garlic in hot oil for about one minute before mixing it with vinegar in a bowl.
- Stir in tomatoes, Parmesan cheese, broccoli, bell pepper, olives, and Romano cheese before refrigerating it for at least an hour.

Serving: 4

Timing Information:

Preparation	Cooking	Total Time
15 mins	15 mins	30 mins

Nutritional Information:

Calories	653 kcal
Carbohydrates	66.9 g
Cholesterol	63 mg
Fat	31.7 g
Fiber	8.1 g
Protein	28 g
Sodium	902 mg

* Percent Daily Values are based on a 2,000 calorie diet.

MAGGIE'S FAVORITE PASTA SALAD

Ingredients

- 1 (12 ounce) package rotini pasta
- 1 (10 ounce) package frozen peas, thawed
- 1 (8 ounce) can water chestnuts, chopped
- 1 (8 ounce) package imitation crabmeat, coarsely chopped - or more to taste
- 1 cup reduced-fat mayonnaise
- 2 tbsps chopped fresh chives
- 1 tbsp chopped fresh dill

Directions

- Cook pasta in salty boiling water for about 10 minutes until tender before draining it.
- Coat pasta with a mixture of peas, mayonnaise, water chestnuts, imitation crabmeat, chives, and dill very thoroughly.
- Serve.

Serving: 12

Timing Information:

Preparation	Cooking	Total Time
10 mins	10 mins	30 mins

Nutritional Information:

Calories	178 kcal
Carbohydrates	33.6 g
Cholesterol	4 mg
Fat	2 g
Fiber	2.5 g
Protein	6.2 g
Sodium	373 mg

* Percent Daily Values are based on a 2,000 calorie diet.

Classical Potato Salad

Ingredients

- 2 lbs clean, scrubbed new red potatoes
- 6 eggs
- 1 lb bacon
- 1 onion, finely diced
- 1 stalk celery, finely diced
- 2 C. mayonnaise
- salt and pepper to taste

Directions

- Boil your potatoes in water and salt for 20 mins then remove the liquids.
- Once the potatoes are no longer hot, chop them, with the skins.
- Now get your eggs boiling in water for 60 secs, place a lid on the pot, and shut the heat.
- Let the eggs sit for 15 mins. Then remove the shells and dice them.
- Stir fry your bacon until it is crispy then break it into pieces.

- Get a bowl, combine: black pepper, celery, salt, eggs, mayo, onion, and bacon.
- Place a covering of plastic around the bowl and put everything in the fridge for 65 mins.
- Enjoy.

Amount per serving (12 total)

Timing Information:

Preparation	
Cooking	1 h
Total Time	2 h

Nutritional Information:

Calories	430 kcal
Fat	36.9 g
Carbohydrates	16.2g
Protein	9.5 g
Cholesterol	121 mg
Sodium	536 mg

* Percent Daily Values are based on a 2,000 calorie diet.

Pecan Chicken Salad

Ingredients

- 4 C. cubed, cooked chicken meat
- 1 C. mayonnaise
- 1 tsp paprika
- 1 1/2 C. dried cranberries
- 1 C. diced celery
- 2 green onions, diced
- 1/2 C. minced green bell pepper
- 1 C. diced pecans
- 1 tsp seasoning salt
- ground black pepper to taste

Directions

- Get a bowl, combine: seasoned salt, paprika, and mayo. Get this mix smooth then add in: the nuts, celery, onion, bell peppers, and cranberries.
- Mix everything again then add the chicken and black pepper.
- Place the contents in the fridge for 65 mins then serve.
- Enjoy.

Amount per serving (12 total)

Timing Information:

Preparation	
Cooking	15 m
Total Time	15 m

Nutritional Information:

Calories	315 kcal
Fat	23.1 g
Carbohydrates	15.2g
Protein	13.9 g
Cholesterol	42 mg
Sodium	213 mg

* Percent Daily Values are based on a 2,000 calorie diet.

Latin Corn Salad

Ingredients

- 1/3 C. fresh lime juice
- 1/2 C. olive oil
- 1 clove garlic, minced
- 1 tsp salt
- 1/8 tsp ground cayenne pepper
- 2 (15 oz.) cans black beans, rinsed and drained
- 1 1/2 C. frozen corn kernels
- 1 avocado - peeled, pitted and diced
- 1 red bell pepper, diced
- 2 tomatoes, diced
- 6 green onions, thinly sliced
- 1/2 C. diced fresh cilantro

Directions

- Get a mason jar and add in: cayenne, lime juice, salt, garlic, and olive oil.
- Place a lid on the jar tightly and shake everything.
- Now get a large bowl, combine: cilantro, beans, green onions, corn, tomatoes, bell pepper, and avocado.
- Combine in the lime mix then toss the contents.

- Enjoy.

Amount per serving (6 total)

Timing Information:

Preparation	
Cooking	25 m
Total Time	25 m

Nutritional Information:

Calories	391 kcal
Fat	24.5 g
Carbohydrates	35.1g
Protein	10.5 g
Cholesterol	0 mg
Sodium	830 mg

* Percent Daily Values are based on a 2,000 calorie diet.

EGG SALAD

Ingredients

- 8 eggs
- 1/2 C. mayonnaise
- 1 tsp prepared yellow mustard
- 1/4 C. diced green onion
- salt and pepper to taste
- 1/4 tsp paprika

Directions

- Boil your eggs in water for 2 mins then place a lid on the pot and let the contents sit for 15 mins. Once the eggs have cooled remove their shells and dice them.
- Now get a bowl, combine: green onions, eggs, mustard, and mayo.
- Stir the mix until it is smooth then add in the paprika, pepper, and salt.
- Stir the contents again then enjoy with toasted buns.

Amount per serving (4 total)

Timing Information:

Preparation	10 m
Cooking	15 m
Total Time	35 m

Nutritional Information:

Calories	344 kcal
Fat	31.9 g
Carbohydrates	2.3g
Protein	< 13 g
Cholesterol	382 mg
Sodium	1351 mg

* Percent Daily Values are based on a 2,000 calorie diet.

Almond Dijon Salad

Ingredients

- 1 C. sliced almonds
- 3 tbsps red wine vinegar
- 1/3 C. olive oil
- 1/4 C. fresh cranberries
- 1 tbsp Dijon mustard
- 1/2 tsp minced garlic
- 1/2 tsp salt
- 1/2 tsp ground black pepper
- 2 tbsps water
- 1/2 red onion, thinly sliced
- 4 oz. crumbled blue cheese
- 1 lb mixed salad greens

Directions

- Set your oven to 375 degrees before doing anything else.
- Place all your almonds on a cookie sheet and bake them for 7 mins in the oven
- Now puree the following with a food processor: water, vinegar, pepper, oil, salt, garlic, and mustard.

- Get a bowl, combine: the vinegar mix, baked almonds, greens, blue cheese, and onions.
- Enjoy.

Amount per serving (8 total)

Timing Information:

Preparation	15 m
Cooking	5 m
Total Time	20 m

Nutritional Information:

Calories	218 kcal
Fat	19.2 g
Carbohydrates	6.2g
Protein	6.5 g
Cholesterol	11 mg
Sodium	405 mg

* Percent Daily Values are based on a 2,000 calorie diet.

SEATTLE SALAD

Ingredients

- 1/2 C. freshly squeezed lemon juice
- 1/4 C. extra-virgin olive oil
- 2 tsps Dijon mustard
- salt and ground black pepper to taste
- 5 C. water
- 2 C. uncooked wild rice
- 1 tsp butter
- 4 C. finely sliced red cabbage
- 2 large red bell peppers - seeded, cored, and diced
- 2 bulbs fennel, trimmed and diced
- 2 bunches kale, leaves stripped from stems and torn into pieces
- 1/4 lemon, juiced, or to taste

Directions

- Get a bowl, combine: pepper, half C. lemon juice, Dijon, olive oil, and salt.
- Now get your wild rice boiling in water. Once it is boiling add the butter, place a lid on the pot, set the heat to low, and let the rice gently cook for 40 mins.

- Now remove any liquids and cook everything for 7 more mins until no liquid remains.
- Let the rice lose its heat then stir it.
- Get a 2nd bowl, combine: dressing, cabbage, fennel, and bell peppers.
- Lay your kale on top then add the wild rice over the kale.
- Let the salad sit for 7 mins before stirring.
- Now add some extra lemon juice then serve.
- Enjoy.

Amount per serving (12 total)

Timing Information:

Preparation	15 m
Cooking	35 m
Total Time	1 h

Nutritional Information:

Calories	211 kcal
Fat	6 g
Carbohydrates	35.2g
Protein	7.6 g
Cholesterol	< 1 mg
Sodium	< 103 mg

* Percent Daily Values are based on a 2,000 calorie diet.

American Potato Salad

Ingredients

- 5 potatoes
- 3 eggs
- 1 C. diced celery
- 1/2 C. diced onion
- 1/2 C. sweet pickle relish
- 1/4 tsp garlic salt
- 1/4 tsp celery salt
- 1 tbsp prepared mustard
- ground black pepper to taste
- 1/4 C. mayonnaise

Directions

- Boil your potatoes in water and salt for 20 mins. Then remove the skins and chunk them.
- Now get your eggs boiling in water.
- Once the water is boiling, place a lid on the pot, and shut the heat.
- Let the eggs sit for 15 mins. Then once they have cooled remove the shells, and dice them.

- Get a bowl, combine: mayo, potatoes, pepper, eggs, mustard, celery, celery salt, onions, garlic, and relish.
- Place a covering of plastic on the mix and put everything in the fridge until it is cold.
- Enjoy.

Amount per serving (8 total)

Timing Information:

Preparation	45 m
Cooking	15 m
Total Time	1 h

Nutritional Information:

Calories	206 kcal
Fat	7.6 g
Carbohydrates	30.5g
Protein	5.5 g
Cholesterol	72 mg
Sodium	335 mg

* Percent Daily Values are based on a 2,000 calorie diet.

Tarragon Wild Rice Salad

Ingredients

- 1 1/2 C. uncooked wild rice
- 6 C. water
- 1/3 C. tarragon vinegar
- 3 tbsps Dijon mustard
- 1 tbsp white sugar
- 1 tsp salt
- 1 clove garlic, minced
- 1 tsp dried tarragon, crumbled
- 1/2 tsp black pepper
- 1/2 tsp crushed red pepper flakes
- 2/3 C. safflower oil
- 3 C. cubed cooked chicken
- 1 C. sliced celery
- 1/2 C. diced fresh parsley
- 1/2 C. sliced green onion
- 1/2 lb sugar snap peas, strings removed
- 1/2 C. toasted slivered almonds

Directions

- Get your rice boiling in water, place a lid on the pot, set the heat to low, and let the rice cook for 35 mins.
- Remove any extra liquids, and stir the rice.
- Let the rice continue to cook for 7 more mins to remove all the liquids. Then add the rice to a bowl.
- Get a 2nd bowl, combine: pepper flakes, vinegar, black pepper, mustard, tarragon, sugar, garlic, and salt.
- Add the safflower oil and whisk the contents until everything is smooth.
- Now add the following to your rice: green onions, chicken, parsley, and celery.
- Add in the wet oil mix then stir everything.
- Place a covering of plastic over the mix and put everything in the fridge for 5 hrs.
- Now begin to boil your peas in water and salt for 1 min.
- Remove the liquids and run them under cold water. Once the peas are chilled slice them diagonally.
- Combine the almonds and the peas with the rice mix and stir the contents evenly then serve the salad.
- Enjoy.

Amount per serving (10 total)

Timing Information:

Preparation	25 m
Cooking	20 m
Total Time	5 h 15 m

Nutritional Information:

Calories	326 kcal
Fat	20.7 g
Carbohydrates	19.2g
Protein	15.9 g
Cholesterol	32 mg
Sodium	390 mg

* Percent Daily Values are based on a 2,000 calorie diet.

Quinoa Pepper Salad

Ingredients

- 1 tsp canola oil
- 1 tbsp minced garlic
- 1/4 C. diced (yellow or purple) onion
- 2 1/2 C. water
- 2 tsps salt, or to taste
- 1/4 tsp ground black pepper
- 2 C. quinoa
- 3/4 C. diced fresh tomato
- 3/4 C. diced carrots
- 1/2 C. diced yellow bell pepper
- 1/2 C. diced cucumber
- 1/2 C. frozen corn kernels, thawed
- 1/4 C. diced red onion
- 1 1/2 tbsps diced fresh cilantro
- 1 tbsp diced fresh mint
- 1 tsp salt
- 1/4 tsp ground black pepper
- 2 tbsps olive oil
- 3 tbsps balsamic vinegar

Directions

- Stir fry 1/4 C. of onions and garlic in canola for 7 mins. Then add in: 1/4 tsp black pepper, water, 2 tsps salt.
- Get everything boiling then add in the quinoa.
- Place a lid on the pot, set the heat to low, and let the quinoa cook for 22 mins.
- Remove any excess liquids, place the mix in a bowl, and put everything in the fridge until it is cold, with a covering of plastic.
- Once the quinoa is cooled combine it with the following: 1/4 tsp black pepper, 1/4 C. red onions, 1 tsp salt, tomato, mint, corn, cilantro, carrots, cucumber, and bell peppers.
- Top the mix with balsamic and olive oil then stir the contents evenly.
- Enjoy.

Amount per serving (12 total)

Timing Information:

Preparation	20 m
Cooking	25 m
Total Time	1 h 30 m

Nutritional Information:

Calories	148 kcal
Fat	4.5 g
Carbohydrates	22.9g
Protein	4.6 g
Cholesterol	0 mg
Sodium	592 mg

* Percent Daily Values are based on a 2,000 calorie diet.

Asparagus Salad

Ingredients

- 1 lb fresh green beans, trimmed and cut into bite-size pieces
- 1 tbsp extra-virgin olive oil
- 1 lb fresh asparagus, trimmed and cut into bite-size pieces
- 1 tbsp extra-virgin olive oil
- 1/2 red onion, diced
- 2 C. cherry tomatoes, halved
- 1/4 C. diced fresh parsley
- kosher salt to taste
- ground black pepper to taste

Directions

- Set your oven to 400 degrees before doing anything else.
- Get a bowl, combine: olive oil (1 tbsp) and green beans.
- Layer the beans onto a cookie sheet and bake everything in the oven for 12 mins.
- Now combine your asparagus with 1 tbsp of olive oil, in the same bowl, then layer them on the same cookie sheet with the green beans.
- Cook the asparagus and beans for 12 more mins.

- Now in the same bowl, combine: parsley, black pepper, green beans, cherry tomatoes, kosher salt, asparagus, and red onions.
- Enjoy.

Amount per serving (8 total)

Timing Information:

Preparation	15 m
Cooking	20 m
Total Time	35 m

Nutritional Information:

Calories	71 kcal
Fat	3.7 g
Carbohydrates	8.8g
Protein	2.7 g
Cholesterol	0 mg
Sodium	59 mg

* Percent Daily Values are based on a 2,000 calorie diet.

Ranch Pasta Salad

Ingredients

- 1 (12 oz.) package uncooked tri-color rotini pasta
- 10 slices bacon
- 1 C. mayonnaise
- 3 tbsps dry ranch salad dressing mix
- 1/4 tsp garlic powder
- 1/2 tsp garlic pepper
- 1/2 C. milk, or as needed
- 1 large tomato, diced
- 1 (4.25 oz.) can sliced black olives
- 1 C. shredded sharp Cheddar cheese

Directions

- Boil your pasta in water and salt for 9 mins, then remove the liquids.
- Stir fry your bacon then break it into pieces once it becomes crispy.
- Get a bowl, combine: garlic pepper, mayo, garlic powder, ranch dressing mix, and milk.
- Stir the contents then add in: cheese, rotini, black olives, bacon, and tomatoes.

- Stir the contents again until everything is smooth then place a covering of plastic around the bowl and put everything in the fridge for 65 mins.
- If the salad is too dry add a bit more milk, if needed.
- Enjoy.

Amount per serving (10 total)

Timing Information:

Preparation	10 m
Cooking	15 m
Total Time	1 h 25 m

Nutritional Information:

Calories	336 kcal
Fat	26.8 g
Carbohydrates	14.9g
Protein	9.3 g
Cholesterol	31 mg
Sodium	691 mg

* Percent Daily Values are based on a 2,000 calorie diet.

STRAWBERRY SESAME SALAD

Ingredients

- 2 tbsps sesame seeds
- 1 tbsp poppy seeds
- 1/2 C. white sugar
- 1/2 C. olive oil
- 1/4 C. distilled white vinegar
- 1/4 tsp paprika
- 1/4 tsp Worcestershire sauce
- 1 tbsp minced onion
- 10 oz. fresh spinach - rinsed, dried and torn into bite-size pieces
- 1 quart strawberries - cleaned, hulled and sliced
- 1/4 C. almonds, blanched and slivered

Directions

- Get a bowl, combine: onion, sesame seeds, Worcestershire, poppy seeds, paprika, sugar, vinegar, and olive oil.
- Place a covering of plastic around the bowl, and put everything in the fridge for 65 mins.

- Get a 2nd bowl, combine: almonds, spinach, and strawberries.
- Combine both bowls and place the combined mix in the fridge for 20 mins.
- Enjoy.

Amount per serving (4 total)

Timing Information:

Preparation	
Cooking	10 m
Total Time	1 h 10 m

Nutritional Information:

Calories	491 kcal
Fat	35.2 g
Carbohydrates	42.9g
Protein	6 g
Cholesterol	0 mg
Sodium	63 mg

* Percent Daily Values are based on a 2,000 calorie diet.

Mediterranean Salad

Ingredients

- 3 cucumbers, seeded and sliced
- 1 1/2 C. crumbled feta cheese
- 1 C. black olives, pitted and sliced
- 3 C. diced roma tomatoes
- 1/3 C. diced oil packed sun-dried tomatoes, drained, oil reserved
- 1/2 red onion, sliced

Directions

- Get a bowl, combine: 2 tbsps sun dried tomato oil, red onions, cucumbers, sundried tomatoes, feta, roma tomatoes, and olives.
- Place a covering of plastic around the bowl and put everything in the fridge until it is cold.
- Enjoy.

Amount per serving (8 total)

Timing Information:

Preparation	
Cooking	10 m
Total Time	10 m

Nutritional Information:

Calories	131 kcal
Fat	8.8 g
Carbohydrates	9.3g
Protein	5.5 g
Cholesterol	25 mg
Sodium	486 mg

* Percent Daily Values are based on a 2,000 calorie diet.

Cranberry Salad

Ingredients

- 1 tbsp butter
- 3/4 C. almonds, blanched and slivered
- 1 lb spinach, rinsed and torn into bite-size pieces
- 1 C. dried cranberries
- 2 tbsps toasted sesame seeds
- 1 tbsp poppy seeds
- 1/2 C. white sugar
- 2 tsps minced onion
- 1/4 tsp paprika
- 1/4 C. white wine vinegar
- 1/4 C. cider vinegar
- 1/2 C. vegetable oil

Directions

- Toast your almonds in butter for 7 mins then place them to the side.
- Get a bowl, combine: veggie oil, sesame seeds, cider vinegar, poppy seeds, wine vinegar, sugar, paprika, and onions.

- Combine in the cranberries, almonds, and spinach and toss the contents.
- Enjoy.

Amount per serving (8 total)

Timing Information:

Preparation	10 m
Cooking	10 m
Total Time	20 m

Nutritional Information:

Calories	338 kcal
Fat	23.5 g
Carbohydrates	30.4g
Protein	4.9 g
Cholesterol	4 mg
Sodium	58 mg

* Percent Daily Values are based on a 2,000 calorie diet.

Mexican Salad

Ingredients

- 1 (15 oz.) can black beans, rinsed and drained
- 1 (15 oz.) can kidney beans, drained
- 1 (15 oz.) can cannellini beans, drained and rinsed
- 1 green bell pepper, diced
- 1 red bell pepper, diced
- 1 (10 oz.) package frozen corn kernels
- 1 red onion, diced
- 1/2 C. olive oil
- 1/2 C. red wine vinegar
- 2 tbsps fresh lime juice
- 1 tbsp lemon juice
- 2 tbsps white sugar
- 1 tbsp salt
- 1 clove crushed garlic
- 1/4 C. diced fresh cilantro
- 1/2 tbsp ground cumin
- 1/2 tbsp ground black pepper
- 1 dash hot pepper sauce
- 1/2 tsp chili powder

Directions

- Get a bowl, combine: red onions, beans, frozen corn, and bell pepper.
- Get a 2nd bowl, combine: black pepper, olive oil, garlic, chili powder, cumin, red vinegar, salt, hot sauce, cilantro, lime juice, sugar, and lemon juice.
- Now combine both bowls, and put everything in the fridge until it is cold.
- Enjoy.

Amount per serving (8 total)

Timing Information:

Preparation	
Cooking	15 m
Total Time	1 h 15 m

Nutritional Information:

Calories	334 kcal
Fat	14.8 g
Carbohydrates	41.7g
Protein	11.2 g
Cholesterol	0 mg
Sodium	1159 mg

* Percent Daily Values are based on a 2,000 calorie diet.

Macaroni Salad

Ingredients

- 4 C. uncooked elbow macaroni
- 1 C. mayonnaise
- 1/4 C. distilled white vinegar
- 2/3 C. white sugar
- 2 1/2 tbsps prepared yellow mustard
- 1 1/2 tsps salt
- 1/2 tsp ground black pepper
- 1 large onion, diced
- 2 stalks celery, diced
- 1 green bell pepper, seeded and diced
- 1/4 C. grated carrot
- 2 tbsps diced pimento peppers

Directions

- Boil your macaroni in water and salt for 9 mins then remove the liquids.
- Get a bowl, combine: macaroni, onions, pimentos, celery, carrots, black pepper, mayo, salt, green peppers, vinegar, mustard, and sugar.

- Place a covering of plastic around the bowl and put everything in the fridge for 5 hrs.
- Enjoy.

Amount per serving (10 total)

Timing Information:

Preparation	20 m
Cooking	10 m
Total Time	4 h 30 m

Nutritional Information:

Calories	390 kcal
Fat	18.7 g
Carbohydrates	49.3g
Protein	6.8 g
Cholesterol	8 mg
Sodium	529 mg

* Percent Daily Values are based on a 2,000 calorie diet.

EASY SPINACH SALAD

Ingredients

- 2 bunches spinach, rinsed and torn into bite-size pieces
- 4 C. sliced strawberries
- 1/2 C. vegetable oil
- 1/4 C. white wine vinegar
- 1/2 C. white sugar
- 1/4 tsp paprika
- 2 tbsps sesame seeds
- 1 tbsp poppy seeds

Directions

- Get a bowl, combine: strawberries and spinach.
- Get a 2nd bowl, combine: poppy seeds, oil, sesame seeds, vinegar, paprika, and sugar.
- Combine both bowls then serve the salad.
- Enjoy.

Amount per serving (8 total)

Timing Information:

Preparation	
Cooking	10 m
Total Time	10 m

Nutritional Information:

Calories	235 kcal
Fat	15.9 g
Carbohydrates	22.8g
Protein	3.6 g
Cholesterol	0 mg
Sodium	69 mg

* Percent Daily Values are based on a 2,000 calorie diet.

Pear and Cheese Salad

Ingredients

- 1 head leaf lettuce, torn into bite-size pieces
- 3 pears - peeled, cored and diced
- 5 oz. Roquefort cheese, crumbled
- 1 avocado - peeled, pitted, and diced
- 1/2 C. thinly sliced green onions
- 1/4 C. white sugar
- 1/2 C. pecans
- 1/3 C. olive oil
- 3 tbsps red wine vinegar
- 1 1/2 tsps white sugar
- 1 1/2 tsps prepared mustard
- 1 clove garlic, diced
- 1/2 tsp salt
- fresh ground black pepper to taste

Directions

- Toast your pecans and 1/4 C. of sugar, while stirring, until the sugar melts and coats the pecans.
- Then place the pecans on some parchment paper.

- Blend the following in a blender until smooth: pepper, oil, salt, 1.5 tsp sugar, diced garlic, and mustard.
- Get a bowl, combine: green onions, lettuce, avocados, pears, blue cheese, and dressing mix.
- Stir the contents then add in your pecans.
- Enjoy.

Amount per serving (6 total)

Timing Information:

Preparation	20 m
Cooking	10 m
Total Time	30 m

Nutritional Information:

Calories	426 kcal
Fat	31.6 g
Carbohydrates	33.1g
Protein	8 g
Cholesterol	21 mg
Sodium	654 mg

* Percent Daily Values are based on a 2,000 calorie diet.

TUNA SALAD

Ingredients

- 1 (7 oz.) can white tuna, drained and flaked
- 6 tbsps mayonnaise or salad dressing
- 1 tbsp Parmesan cheese
- 3 tbsps sweet pickle relish
- 1/8 tsp dried minced onion flakes
- 1/4 tsp curry powder
- 1 tbsp dried parsley
- 1 tsp dried dill weed
- 1 pinch garlic powder

Directions

- Get a bowl, combine: onion flakes, tuna, parmesan, and mayo.
- Stir the contents until they are smooth then add the garlic powder, curry powder, dill, and parsley.
- Stir the contents again to evenly distribute the spices.
- Enjoy over toasted buns or crackers.

Amount per serving (4 total)

Timing Information:

Preparation	
Cooking	10 m
Total Time	10 m

Nutritional Information:

Calories	228 kcal
Fat	17.3 g
Carbohydrates	5.3g
Protein	13.4 g
Cholesterol	24 mg
Sodium	255 mg

* Percent Daily Values are based on a 2,000 calorie diet.

Broccoli Sunflower Salad

Ingredients

- 10 slices bacon
- 1 head fresh broccoli, cut into bite size pieces
- 1/4 C. red onion, diced
- 1/2 C. raisins
- 3 tbsps white wine vinegar
- 2 tbsps white sugar
- 1 C. mayonnaise
- 1 C. sunflower seeds

Directions

- Stir fry your bacon until crispy then break it into pieces.
- Get a bowl, combine: raisins, broccoli, and onions.
- Get a 2nd bowl, combine: mayo, sugar, and vinegar.
- Combine both bowls then place a covering of plastic around the bowl.
- Put everything in the fridge for 4 hours.
- Add in your bacon and stir the salad. Then add the sunflower seeds as a topping.
- Enjoy.

Amount per serving (6 total)

Timing Information:

Preparation	15 m
Cooking	15 m
Total Time	4 h 30 m

Nutritional Information:

Calories	559 kcal
Fat	48.1 g
Carbohydrates	23.9g
Protein	12.9 g
Cholesterol	31 mg
Sodium	584 mg

* Percent Daily Values are based on a 2,000 calorie diet.

Caesar

Ingredients

- 6 cloves garlic, peeled
- 3/4 C. mayonnaise
- 5 anchovy fillets, minced
- 6 tbsps grated Parmesan cheese, divided
- 1 tsp Worcestershire sauce
- 1 tsp Dijon mustard
- 1 tbsp lemon juice
- salt to taste
- ground black pepper to taste
- 1/4 C. olive oil
- 4 C. day-old bread, cubed
- 1 head romaine lettuce, torn into bite-size pieces

Directions

- Dice 3 pieces of garlic and add them to a bowl with: Worcestershire, lemon juice, mayo, 2 tbsp parmesan, mustard, and anchovies.
- Slice the rest of the garlic in quarters then stir fry them in hot oil until browned. Then place them to the side.

- Add the bread pieces into the pot and brown them while stirring.
- Top the bread with pepper and salt and place everything in a bowl.
- Combine the following with the bread: parmesan, lettuce, and Worcestershire mix.
- Enjoy.

Amount per serving (6 total)

Timing Information:

Preparation	20 m
Cooking	15 m
Total Time	35 m

Nutritional Information:

Calories	384 kcal
Fat	33.5 g
Carbohydrates	16.3g
Protein	5.8 g
Cholesterol	18 mg
Sodium	549 mg

* Percent Daily Values are based on a 2,000 calorie diet.

Couscous Salad

Ingredients

- 1 C. uncooked couscous
- 1 1/4 C. chicken broth
- 3 tbsps extra virgin olive oil
- 2 tbsps fresh lime juice
- 1 tsp red wine vinegar
- 1/2 tsp ground cumin
- 8 green onions, diced
- 1 red bell pepper, seeded and diced
- 1/4 C. diced fresh cilantro
- 1 C. frozen corn kernels, thawed
- 2 (15 oz.) cans black beans, drained
- salt and pepper to taste

Directions

- Get your broth boiling, then add in the couscous.
- Place a lid on the pot and let the contents sit for 7 mins.
- Get a bowl, combine: beans, olive oil, corn, lime juice, cilantro, vinegar, red pepper, cumin, and green onions.
- Toss the contents, then stir your couscous.

- Add the couscous in with the beans and corn. Then stir the mix again.
- Add some pepper and salt then place the contents in the fridge for 10 mins.
- Enjoy.

Amount per serving (8 total)

Timing Information:

Preparation	
Cooking	30 m
Total Time	45 m

Nutritional Information:

Calories	255 kcal
Fat	5.9 g
Carbohydrates	41.2g
Protein	10.4 g
Cholesterol	< 1 mg
Sodium	< 565 mg

* Percent Daily Values are based on a 2,000 calorie diet.

Monarch Ranch Fruit Juice Salad

Ingredients

- 1 C. green grapes, some halved and some whole
- 8 fresh strawberries, chopped
- 1 fresh plum, core removed, chopped
- 1/2 C. fresh blackberries
- 1/2 Granny Smith apple, chopped
- 1/2 orange, juiced

Directions

- Get a salad bowl, gently toss: apple, grapes, blackberries, plums, and strawberries. Combine in your orange juice and toss everything once more.
- Enjoy.

Amount per serving 4
Timing Information:

Preparation	10 m
Total Time	10 m

Nutritional Information:

Calories	69 kcal
Fat	0.4 g
Carbohydrates	< 17.2g
Protein	0.8 g
Cholesterol	0 mg
Sodium	3 mg

* Percent Daily Values are based on a 2,000 calorie diet.

Michelle's Favorites

Ingredients

- 1 29 oz. can pear slices, drained and cut into bite-size pieces
- 1 28 oz. can sliced peaches, drained and cut into bite-size pieces with 1 C. liquid reserved
- 1 20 oz. can pineapple tidbits, drained
- 1 4.6 oz. package non-instant vanilla pudding mix

Directions

- Get a bowl, combine: pineapple, peaches, and pears.
- In a pot add in the pudding mix and juice from the peaches and with a low level of heat stir and warm the mix for 7 mins. Combine this mix with the fruits and toss everything gently.
- Place a covering of plastic on the bowl and put everything in the fridge for 30 mins.
- Enjoy.

Amount per serving 8
Timing Information:

Preparation	10 m
Cooking	5 m
Total Time	35 m

Nutritional Information:

Calories	199 kcal
Fat	0.2 g
Carbohydrates	< 51g
Protein	1.3 g
Cholesterol	0 mg
Sodium	130 mg

* Percent Daily Values are based on a 2,000 calorie diet.

SUNFLOWER HEALTHY LUNCH

Ingredients

- 2 C. mixed salad greens
- 1/4 C. ranch dressing
- 3/4 C. diced tomato
- 3/4 C. dried cranberries
- 1/2 C. sunflower seeds
- 1/3 C. almonds
- 2 tbsps flax seeds
- 1/3 tsp sea salt
- 1/4 tsp chopped garlic
- 2 tbsps grated Parmesan cheese, or to taste

Directions

- Get a salad bowl, combine: dressing and greens. Toss the greens to get them mixed well. Combine in the garlic, tomato, sea salt, cranberries, flax seeds, almonds, and sunflower seeds. Toss the salad gently then garnish everything with the parmesan and stir.
- Enjoy.

Amount per serving 8
Timing Information:

Preparation	10 m
Total Time	10 m

Nutritional Information:

Calories	184 kcal
Fat	13.2 g
Carbohydrates	14.6g
Protein	4.6 g
Cholesterol	3 mg
Sodium	170 mg

* Percent Daily Values are based on a 2,000 calorie diet.

Coconut Cantaloupe

Ingredients

- 1 cantaloupe - peeled, seeded, and cubed
- 2 red apples, thinly sliced
- 1 C. red grapes
- 1 12 oz. can mandarin oranges in juice
- 1/4 C. sweetened flaked coconut optional

Directions

- Get a salad bowl and layer in it half of the following: cantaloupe, mandarins, apple, and grapes. Continue add the rest of ingredients in the same manner.
- Add your coconut over everything as a topping.

Amount per serving 8
Timing Information:

Preparation	15 m
Total Time	15 m

Nutritional Information:

Calories	82 kcal
Fat	1 g
Carbohydrates	19.2g
Protein	1.1 g
Cholesterol	0 mg
Sodium	21 mg

* Percent Daily Values are based on a 2,000 calorie diet.

Complex Southern Fruit Salad

Ingredients

- 3 bananas, peeled and cut into chunks
- 1 13.25 oz. can pineapple chunks, drained
- 2 red apples, cored and cut into bite-sized pieces
- 2 Granny Smith apples, cored and cut into bite-sized pieces
- 2 kiwi fruit, peeled and cut into chunks
- 3 oranges - peeled, segmented, and cut into bite-sized pieces
- 2 tangerines, peeled and segmented
- 1 C. mayonnaise
- 1 4 oz. jar maraschino cherries, drained and juice reserved
- 1/2 8 oz. package chopped walnuts, or to taste
- 1/2 C. chopped celery, or more to taste
    - 1/2 3.5 oz. package sweetened flaked coconut, or more to taste

Directions

- Get a bowl, combine: coconut, bananas, celery, pineapple, walnuts, red apples, cherries, granny smith, mayo, kiwi, tangerines, and oranges.
- Toss the salad gently then add in the cherry juice that was reserved and toss everything again. Place a covering on the bowl and put everything in the fridge for 1 hr.

- Enjoy.

Amount per serving 10
Timing Information:

Preparation	25 m
Total Time	55 m

Nutritional Information:

Calories	398 kcal
Fat	27.1 g
Carbohydrates	40.6g
Protein	3.7 g
Cholesterol	8 mg
Sodium	151 mg

* Percent Daily Values are based on a 2,000 calorie diet.

JUICE BAR FRUIT SALAD DRINK

Ingredients

- 2 C. milk
- 1 8 oz. can pineapple tidbits
- 1 apple, chopped
- 1 pear, chopped
- 4 strawberries, chopped
- 1/4 C. cherries, pitted and chopped, or to taste
- 2 tbsps vanilla yogurt, or more to taste

Directions

- Add the following to your food processor and puree it: yogurt, milk, cherries, pineapple, strawberries, pear and apple.
- Once the mix is smoothie like, should be 6 mins of processing, pour the smoothies into serving glasses, recipes makes about 6 servings.
- Enjoy.

Amount per serving 6
Timing Information:

Preparation	10 m
Total Time	10 m

Nutritional Information:

Calories	104 kcal
Fat	1.9 g
Carbohydrates	19.7g
Protein	3.4 g
Cholesterol	7 mg
Sodium	38 mg

* Percent Daily Values are based on a 2,000 calorie diet.

Vegetarian Tofu Fruit Salad Lunch

Ingredients

- 1/2 C. white rice
- 2 C. extra-firm tofu, drained and cubed
- 1 C. yogurt
- 2 tbsps lime juice
- 1 tbsp curry powder
- 1 C. halved grapes
- 1 tbsp dried cranberries
- 1/2 C. diced celery
- 3 tbsps diced green onions
- 1/4 C. walnuts
- salt and pepper to taste

Directions

- Get your water boiling in a larger pot then once it is add in the rice. Place a lid on the pot, set the heat to low, and let everything cook for 22 mins, then shut the heat.
- Begin to get another pan of water boiling then place your tofu in it to cook for 4 mins. Remove all the liquid and let the tofu lose its heat.

- Get a bowl, combine: curry powder, lime juice, and yogurt. Work the mix until it is completely combined.
- Now get a 2nd bigger bowl, combine: tofu, grapes, rice, cranberries, walnuts, green onions, and celery.
- Toss the rice fruit salad with your lime dressing then add some pepper and salt.
- Enjoy.

Amount per serving 8
Timing Information:

Preparation	30 m
Cooking	25 m
Total Time	55 m

Nutritional Information:

Calories	168 kcal
Fat	6.9 g
Carbohydrates	19.2g
Protein	9.6 g
Cholesterol	2 mg
Sodium	< 325 mg

* Percent Daily Values are based on a 2,000 calorie diet.

Apricots and Lemon Fruit Salad with Nuts

Ingredients

- 1 3 oz. package lemon pudding mix
- 1 15.5 oz. can mandarin oranges, drained with liquid reserved
- 3 bananas, sliced
- 1 C. sliced apricots
- 1 kiwis, peeled and sliced optional
- 1/2 C. chopped cashews optional

Directions

- Get a bowl and mix the juice from the oranges with the pudding mix. Work the mix until it smooth then combine in the cashews, bananas, kiwi, and apricots. Place a covering of plastic on the bowl and put everything in the fridge until it is cold.
- Enjoy.

Amount per serving 8
Timing Information:

Preparation	20 m
Total Time	50 m

Nutritional Information:

Calories	232 kcal
Fat	5.3 g
Carbohydrates	46.2g
Protein	1.7 g
Cholesterol	0 mg
Sodium	190 mg

* Percent Daily Values are based on a 2,000 calorie diet.

Autumn Cinnamon Salad

Ingredients

- 8 prunes pitted prunes
- 1/4 C. dried apricots
- 1 C. apple juice
- 1 cinnamon stick
- 1/2 tsp whole cloves
- 1 banana, peeled and sliced
- 1 large orange, peeled, sectioned, and cut into bite-size
- 1 apple, cored and chopped
- 1/2 C. orange juice
- 3 tbsps orange marmalade
- 1/4 C. chopped pecans

Directions

- Get the following boiling in pot: cloves, prunes, cinnamon, apple juice, and apricots. Once the mix is boiling shut the heat and let the mix stand for about 7 hours.
- Take out the dried fruit from the mix then separate the orange, prunes, banana, and apricots between 4 serving platters.

- Run the orange marmalade, orange juice, and apple juice from a strainer then garnish the servings with the resulting liquid.
- Garnish each serving finally with the nuts.
- Enjoy.

Amount per serving 4
Timing Information:

Preparation	15 m
Cooking	10 m
Total Time	13 h 45 m

Nutritional Information:

Calories	263 kcal
Fat	5.4 g
Carbohydrates	55.9g
Protein	2.6 g
Cholesterol	0 mg
Sodium	13 mg

* Percent Daily Values are based on a 2,000 calorie diet.

Fruit Salad Sauce

Ingredients

- 8 oz. sour cream
- 1 14 oz. can sweetened condensed milk
- 1 tsp vanilla extract
- 1/2 tsp almond extract
- 1/4 tsp ground cinnamon, or to taste
- 1/4 tsp ground cardamom, or to taste

Directions

- Get a bowl, combine: cardamom, sour cream, cinnamon, condensed milk, almond extract, and vanilla. Whisk the mix completely then place a covering of plastic on the bowl and put everything in the fridge as a dressing for any salad of fruit.
- Enjoy.

Amount per serving 16
Timing Information:

Preparation	5 m
Total Time	5 m

Nutritional Information:

Calories	110 kcal
Fat	5.1 g
Carbohydrates	14g
Protein	2.4 g
Cholesterol	15 mg
Sodium	39 mg

* Percent Daily Values are based on a 2,000 calorie diet.

Strawberry Sesame Salad

Ingredients

- 2 tbsps sesame seeds
- 1 tbsp poppy seeds
- 1/2 C. white sugar
- 1/2 C. olive oil
- 1/4 C. distilled white vinegar
- 1/4 tsp paprika
- 1/4 tsp Worcestershire sauce
- 1 tbsp minced onion
- 10 oz. fresh spinach - rinsed, dried and torn into bite-size pieces
- 1 quart strawberries - cleaned, hulled and sliced
- 1/4 C. almonds, blanched and slivered

Directions

- Get a bowl, combine: onion, sesame seeds, Worcestershire, poppy seeds, paprika, sugar, vinegar, and olive oil.
- Place a covering of plastic around the bowl, and put everything in the fridge for 65 mins.

- Get a 2nd bowl, combine: almonds, spinach, and strawberries.
- Combine both bowls and place the combined mix in the fridge for 20 mins.
- Enjoy.

Amount per serving (4 total)

Timing Information:

Preparation	
Cooking	10 m
Total Time	1 h 10 m

Nutritional Information:

Calories	491 kcal
Fat	35.2 g
Carbohydrates	42.9g
Protein	6 g
Cholesterol	0 mg
Sodium	63 mg

* Percent Daily Values are based on a 2,000 calorie diet.

CRANBERRY SALAD

Ingredients

- 1 tbsp butter
- 3/4 C. almonds, blanched and slivered
- 1 lb spinach, rinsed and torn into bite-size pieces
- 1 C. dried cranberries
- 2 tbsps toasted sesame seeds
- 1 tbsp poppy seeds
- 1/2 C. white sugar
- 2 tsps minced onion
- 1/4 tsp paprika
- 1/4 C. white wine vinegar
- 1/4 C. cider vinegar
- 1/2 C. vegetable oil

Directions

- Toast your almonds in butter for 7 mins then place them to the side.
- Get a bowl, combine: veggie oil, sesame seeds, cider vinegar, poppy seeds, wine vinegar, sugar, paprika, and onions.

- Combine in the cranberries, almonds, and spinach and toss the contents.
- Enjoy.

Amount per serving (8 total)

Timing Information:

Preparation	10 m
Cooking	10 m
Total Time	20 m

Nutritional Information:

Calories	338 kcal
Fat	23.5 g
Carbohydrates	30.4g
Protein	4.9 g
Cholesterol	4 mg
Sodium	58 mg

* Percent Daily Values are based on a 2,000 calorie diet.

ORANGE ROMAINE SALAD

Ingredients

- 1/2 C. orange juice
- 3 tbsps olive oil
- 2 tbsps red wine vinegar
- 1/2 tsp ground black pepper
- 1/4 tsp salt
- 1 large head romaine lettuce - torn, washed and dried
- 3 (11 oz.) cans mandarin oranges
- 1/2 C. slivered almonds

Directions

- Get a bowl, combine: salt, orange juice, pepper, olive oil, and vinegar.
- Get a 2nd bigger bowl, combine: orange and romaine.
- Combine both bowls and add the almonds.
- Enjoy.

Amount per serving (4 total)

Timing Information:

Preparation	
Cooking	15 m
Total Time	15 m

Nutritional Information:

Calories	332 kcal
Fat	16.7 g
Carbohydrates	47g
Protein	4.9 g
Cholesterol	0 mg
Sodium	168 mg

* Percent Daily Values are based on a 2,000 calorie diet.

CHINESE ORANGE SALAD

Ingredients

- 1/2 C. vegetable oil
- 1/4 C. cider vinegar
- 1/4 C. white sugar
- 2 tsps dried parsley
- 1 tsp salt
- 1 pinch ground black pepper
- 1/2 C. sliced almonds
- 1/4 C. white sugar
- 1 head red leaf lettuce - rinsed, dried and torn
- 1 red onion, diced
- 1 C. diced celery
- 2 (11 oz.) cans mandarin orange segments, drained

Directions

- Get a Mason jar, combine: pepper, oil, salt, vinegar, parsley, and sugar.
- Place a lid on the jar and shake the contents. Then put everything in the fridge.
- Toast your almonds with the sugar until the sugar melts and coats the nuts.

- Let the almonds cool then break them into pieces.
- Get a bowl, combine: almonds, lettuce, orange, and celery. Add in the dressing and stir the mix to evenly distribute the dressing.
- Enjoy.

Amount per serving (5 total)

Timing Information:

Preparation	
Cooking	25 m
Total Time	25 m

Nutritional Information:

Calories	397 kcal
Fat	26.8 g
Carbohydrates	38.2g
Protein	4 g
Cholesterol	0 mg
Sodium	509 mg

* Percent Daily Values are based on a 2,000 calorie diet.

Peach Yogurt Salad

Ingredients

- 3 large peaches, peeled and cut into chunks
- 1 1/2 C. blueberries
- 1 1/2 C. sliced strawberries
- 2 bananas, sliced
- 3 tsps lemon juice

Orange-Yogurt Sauce:

- 1 C. vanilla nonfat or low-fat yogurt
- 2 tbsps frozen orange juice concentrate

Directions

- Get a bowl, combine: lemon juice and fruit.
- Get a 2nd bowl, combine: concentrate and yogurt.
- Combine both bowls and add a garnishing of mint.
- Enjoy.

Amount per serving (6 total)

Timing Information:

Preparation	10 m
Cooking	
Total Time	10 m

Nutritional Information:

Calories	141 kcal
Fat	0.5 g
Carbohydrates	33.2g
Protein	3.3 g
Cholesterol	< 1 mg
Sodium	< 32 mg

* Percent Daily Values are based on a 2,000 calorie diet.

Baltimore Style Coleslaw

Ingredients

- 1/2 C. mayonnaise
- 2 tbsp chopped onion
- 1 tbsp vinegar
- 2 tsp white sugar
- 1 tsp seafood seasoning (such as Old Bay(R))
- 3 C. shredded cabbage
- 1/2 C. shredded carrots
- 1/4 C. chopped green bell pepper

Directions

- In a large salad bowl, add the mayonnaise, onion, vinegar, sugar and seafood seasoning and beat till the sugar is dissolved.
- Add the cabbage, carrots and green bell pepper and stir to combine well.

Amount per serving (8 total)

Timing Information:

Preparation	
Cooking	20 m
Total Time	20 m

Nutritional Information:

Calories	115 kcal
Fat	11 g
Carbohydrates	4.2g
Protein	0.6 g
Cholesterol	5 mg
Sodium	152 mg

* Percent Daily Values are based on a 2,000 calorie diet.

Hot Cross Coleslaw

Ingredients

- 3 tbsp apple cider vinegar
- 3 tbsp canola oil
- 3 tbsp white sugar
- 1/4 tsp dry mustard
- 1/4 tsp poppy seeds
- 1/4 tsp ground black pepper
- 1/4 tsp salt
- 1/4 tsp hot pepper sauce (optional)
- 4 C. shredded green cabbage
- 2 carrots, shredded

Directions

- In a bowl, add the apple cider vinegar, canola oil, sugar, dry mustard, poppy seeds, black pepper, salt and hot pepper and mix till the sugar is dissolved.
- In a large salad bowl, mix together the cabbage and carrots.
- Place the dressing over the slaw and stir to coat.
- Refrigerate for at least 2 hours before serving.

Amount per serving (6 total)

Timing Information:

Preparation	
Cooking	15 m
Total Time	2 h 15 m

Nutritional Information:

Calories	109 kcal
Fat	7.2 g
Carbohydrates	11.1g
Protein	0.9 g
Cholesterol	0 mg
Sodium	125 mg

* Percent Daily Values are based on a 2,000 calorie diet.

THOUSAND ISLAND COLESLAW

Ingredients

- 1 (10 oz.) package angel hair-style shredded cabbage
- 2 tbsp Thousand Island dressing
- 2 tbsp seasoned rice vinegar
- 1 tsp hot sauce
- 1 pinch salt

Directions

- In a bowl, add the cabbage, Thousand Island dressing, rice vinegar, hot sauce and with a fork, mix till well combined.

Amount per serving (6 total)

Timing Information:

Preparation	
Cooking	10 m
Total Time	10 m

Nutritional Information:

Calories	27 kcal
Fat	2 g
Carbohydrates	2.5g
Protein	< 0.1 g
Cholesterol	< 2 mg
Sodium	< 242 mg

* Percent Daily Values are based on a 2,000 calorie diet.

MANILA COLESLAW

Ingredients

- 1/2 small head green cabbage, cored and thinly sliced
- 1/2 jicama, sliced into matchsticks
- 1 large sweet apple (such as Fuji), sliced into matchsticks
- 1/2 C. mayonnaise
- 1/4 C. pineapple juice
- 1 tsp white sugar
- hot sauce to taste
- salt and freshly ground black pepper to taste
- 1/4 bunch chopped fresh cilantro
- 1/3 oz. toasted corn bits (such as Corn Nuts (R)), crushed

Directions

- In a large bowl, mix together the cabbage, jicama, and apple.
- In another bowl, add the mayonnaise, pineapple juice, sugar, hot sauce, salt and pepper and beat till smooth and fluffy.
- Place the mayonnaise mixture over the cabbage, jicama, and apple and toss to coat.
- Keep aside for about 5 minutes.

- Add the cilantro and toss again.
- Serve immediately with a garnishing of the toasted corn bits.

Amount per serving (4 total)

Timing Information:

Preparation	
Cooking	15 m
Total Time	20 m

Nutritional Information:

Calories	302 kcal
Fat	22.5 g
Carbohydrates	25.6g
Protein	2.5 g
Cholesterol	10 mg
Sodium	303 mg

* Percent Daily Values are based on a 2,000 calorie diet.

Couple's Coleslaw

Ingredients

- 1/2 C. mayonnaise
- 1/3 C. white sugar
- 1/4 C. milk
- 2 tbsp lemon juice
- 1 1/2 tbsp white vinegar
- 2 tsp sour cream
- 1/2 tsp freshly ground black pepper
- 1 pinch cayenne pepper, or to taste
- 1 lb. cabbage, cut into wedges
- 2 carrots
- 1/4 small onion, chopped

Directions

- In a bowl, add the mayonnaise, sugar, milk, lemon juice, vinegar, sour cream, black pepper and cayenne pepper and mix till well combined.
- In a food processor, add the cabbage, carrots and onion and with a grater attachment, shred them.
- Transfer the vegetables mixture in a large bowl.
- Add the mayonnaise mixture and stir to combine.

- Refrigerate, covered for at least 2 hours or overnight.
- Stir coleslaw before serving.

Amount per serving (8 total)

Timing Information:

Preparation	
Cooking	15 m
Total Time	2 h 15 m

Nutritional Information:

Calories	160 kcal
Fat	11.4 g
Carbohydrates	14.6g
Protein	1.3 g
Cholesterol	6 mg
Sodium	103 mg

* Percent Daily Values are based on a 2,000 calorie diet.

Bavarian Style Coleslaw

Ingredients

- 1/2 head cabbage, thinly sliced
- 3 tbsp white sugar
- 3 tbsp cider vinegar
- 1/2 tsp celery seed
- 1/2 tsp salt
- 1/2 C. mayonnaise

Directions

- In a large bowl, place the cabbage.
- In another bowl, mix together the sugar, vinegar, celery seed and salt.
- Add the mayonnaise and mix till dressing is smooth and creamy.
- Place the dressing over the cabbage and toss to coat.
- Refrigerator for about 2-3 hours.
- Stir well before serving.

Amount per serving (6 total)

Timing Information:

Preparation	
Cooking	10 m
Total Time	2 h 10 m

Nutritional Information:

Calories	183 kcal
Fat	14.7 g
Carbohydrates	12.7g
Protein	1.5 g
Cholesterol	7 mg
Sodium	316 mg

* Percent Daily Values are based on a 2,000 calorie diet.

Picnic Coleslaw

Ingredients

- 1 (16 oz.) package shredded coleslaw mix
- 2 C. seedless red grapes, halved
- 1/2 C. shredded carrot
- 1 C. mayonnaise
- 1/4 C. prepared Dijon-style mustard
- 1/3 C. crumbled blue cheese
- 2 tbsp white sugar
- 2 tbsp cider vinegar

Directions

- In a large bowl, add mayonnaise, mustard, cheese, sugar and vinegar and beat till well combined.
- Add the coleslaw mix, grapes and carrots and stir till well combined.
- Refrigerate to chill before serving.

Amount per serving (12 total)

Timing Information:

Preparation	
Cooking	10 m
Total Time	10 m

Nutritional Information:

Calories	209 kcal
Fat	16.8 g
Carbohydrates	13.6g
Protein	1.7 g
Cholesterol	13 mg
Sodium	294 mg

* Percent Daily Values are based on a 2,000 calorie diet.

Alabama Inspired Coleslaw

Ingredients

- 1 head cabbage, finely shredded
- 2 carrots, finely chopped
- 2 tbsp finely chopped onion
- 1/2 C. mayonnaise
- 1/3 C. white sugar
- 1/4 C. milk
- 1/4 C. buttermilk
- 2 tbsp lemon juice
- 2 tbsp distilled white vinegar
- 1/2 tsp salt
- 1/8 tsp ground black pepper

Directions

- In a large salad bowl, mix together the cabbage, carrots and onion.
- In another bowl, add the mayonnaise, sugar, milk, buttermilk, lemon juice, vinegar, salt and black pepper and beat till smooth and the sugar is dissolved.
- Place the dressing over cabbage mixture and mix till well combined.

- Refrigerate, covered for at least 2 hours.
- Just before serving, mix again before serving.

Amount per serving (8 total)

Timing Information:

Preparation	
Cooking	20 m
Total Time	2 h 20 m

Nutritional Information:

Calories	184 kcal
Fat	11.3 g
Carbohydrates	20.3g
Protein	2.7 g
Cholesterol	6 mg
Sodium	274 mg

* Percent Daily Values are based on a 2,000 calorie diet.

Rice Vinegar and Lime Coleslaw

Ingredients

- 3/4 C. mayonnaise
- 1 lime, zested
- 2 tsp fresh lime juice
- 1/2 tsp rice vinegar
- 2 cloves garlic, minced
- 2 tsp sweet chili sauce
- 2 tsp white sugar
- 3 tbsp finely chopped fresh cilantro
- 1/4 red onion, finely diced
- 4 C. shredded green cabbage

Directions

- In a large bowl, add the mayonnaise, lime zest, lime juice, rice vinegar, garlic, sweet chili sauce and sugar and mix till the sugar dissolves.
- Add the cilantro and red onion and stir to combine.
- Slowly, add the cabbage about 1 C. at a time, mixing till all the cabbage is coated.

Amount per serving (7 total)

Timing Information:

Preparation	
Cooking	25 m
Total Time	25 m

Nutritional Information:

Calories	189 kcal
Fat	18.8 g
Carbohydrates	5.6g
Protein	0.9 g
Cholesterol	9 mg
Sodium	164 mg

* Percent Daily Values are based on a 2,000 calorie diet.

THANKS FOR READING! JOIN THE CLUB AND KEEP ON COOKING WITH 6 MORE COOKBOOKS....

http://bit.ly/1TdrStv

To grab the box sets simply follow the link mentioned above, or tap one of book covers.

This will take you to a page where you can simply enter your email address and a PDF version of the box sets will be emailed to you.

Hope you are ready for some serious cooking!

http://bit.ly/1TdrStv

Come On...
Let's Be Friends :)

We adore our readers and love connecting with them socially.

Like BookSumo on Facebook and let's get social!

Facebook

And also check out the BookSumo Cooking Blog.

Food Lover Blog

Made in the USA
Coppell, TX
18 November 2019